First Facts®

Christmas around the World

Christmas in the
PHILIPPINES

by Cheryl L. Enderlein

raintree
a Capstone company — publishers for children

Raintree is an imprint of Capstone Global Library Limited, a company incorporated in England and
Wales having its registered office at 264 Banbury Road, Oxford, OX2 7DY – Registered company
number: 6695582

www.raintree.co.uk
myorders@raintree.co.uk

Christine Peterson, editor; Ted Williams, designer; Eric Gohl, media researcher;
Kathy McColley, production specialist

ISBN 978 1 4747 2570 5
20 19 18 17 16
10 9 8 7 6 5 4 3 2 1

British Library Cataloguing in Publication Data
A full catalogue record for this book is available from the British Library.

Acknowledgements
We would like to thank the following for permission to reproduce photographs: AP Images: Aaron
Favila, cover, 17; BigStockPhoto.com: tonyoquias, 6; Capstone Studio: Karon Dubke, 21; Getty
Images: AFP/Ted Aljibe, 20; Newscom: Design Pics, 14, EPA/Dennis M. Sabangan, 1, EPA/Francis
R. Malasig, 9, Getty Images/AFP/Jay Directo, 10, Getty Images/AFP/Luis Liwanag, 13, Getty
Images/AFP/Romeo Gacad, 5; Wikipedia: Kguirnela, 18. Design elements: Shutterstock.

Every effort has been made to contact copyright holders of material reproduced in this book. Any
omissions will be rectified in subsequent printings if notice is given to the publisher.

All the internet addresses (URLs) given in this book were valid at the time of going to press.
However, due to the dynamic nature of the internet, some addresses may have changed, or sites
may have changed or ceased to exist since publication. While the author and publisher regret any
inconvenience this may cause readers, no responsibility for any such changes can be accepted by
either the author or the publisher.

Made in China

CONTENTS

Christmas in the Philippines

Welcome to the Philippines! During Christmas this island country is called the "Land of **Fiestas**". Filipinos say their Christmas celebrations are the longest and most joyful in the world. In this country Christmas celebrations begin on 16 December. The festivities end on the first Sunday in January. This day is known as the "Feast of the **Three Kings**".

fiesta holiday or religious festival, especially in Spanish-speaking countries
Three Kings three kings who are believed to have followed a star to find Jesus in Bethlehem

4

Philippines

How to say it!
In the Philippines, people say *"Maligayang Pasko"*, which means "Merry Christmas".

CHRISTMAS FACT!

It is believed that shepherds and kings followed a bright star to find Jesus.

The first Christmas

Christians celebrate the birth of Jesus at Christmas. They believe that long ago Jesus' parents, Mary and Joseph, travelled to Bethlehem. The town was very crowded. Mary was going to have a baby, but they had nowhere to stay. So they spent the night in a stable, where Jesus was born. Shepherds and kings came to the stable to celebrate his birth.

Christian person who follows a religion based on the teachings of Jesus. Christians believe that Jesus is the son of God.

Christmas celebrations

Church bells mark the start of Christmas in the Philippines. On 16 December bells ring at 4.00 a.m. People get up and go to church. They go to church every day for the next nine days.

On Christmas Eve, people go to midnight mass. When the church service is over, people gather for *Noche Buena*. This celebration lasts all night and includes food, music and gifts.

9

CHRISTMAS FACT!

Filipinos begin making *parols* two or three months before Christmas.

Christmas symbols

Brightly coloured *parols* fill streets and homes in the Philippines during Christmas. A *parol* is a five-pointed star that is often placed inside a circle. *Parols* remind people of the star the Three Kings followed to find Jesus. *Parols* are usually made from **bamboo** and bright paper. Candles or other lights are placed inside *parols*.

bamboo tropical grass with a hard, hollow stem

Christmas decorations

Parols are popular, but Filipinos also decorate Christmas trees. Few **evergreens** grow in the Philippines, so many people have artificial trees. Some use palm tree branches. Others make trees from twigs and cardboard.

People decorate their trees with lights and **ornaments**. Ornaments are often made from fruit, shells and bamboo.

evergreen tree or bush that has green leaves all year round
ornament decoration hung on a Christmas tree

CHRISTMAS FACT!

Father Christmas is not a big part of Christmas in the Philippines. Children there know about him, but he does not bring presents.

Lolo and Lola

Grandparents play a special role in Filipino Christmas celebrations. In the Philippines they are called *Lolo* (grandfather) and *Lola* (grandmother). During a family's holiday feast, Lolo and Lola give gifts to their grandchildren. They usually organize games for children to play. In one game grandparents throw gold coins into the air. The children then rush in to grab the money.

Christmas presents

Christmas gifts in the Philippines are simple and useful. Many people get new clothes that they wear to midnight mass. During the *Noche Buena* celebration, people go from house to house visiting family. Children usually get a small gift at each house. Gifts might be toys, money or sweets.

CHRISTMAS FACT!

Bibingkas are served in a banana leaf. The leaf acts as a plate.

Christmas food

Food covers family tables during Christmas feasts in the Philippines. During *Noche Buena*, at least 15 different foods are served. People enjoy chicken and rice soup. They eat spring rolls stuffed with meat and vegetables. A pancake made with rice flour is a favourite dessert. The pancake, called *bibingka*, is cooked with milk, cheese and duck eggs. It is served with coconut and brown sugar.

Christmas songs

Young and old join together to sing Christmas songs in the Philippines. People sing every night, beginning on 16 December. Groups of children called *cumbancheros* sing as they go from house to house. Some play musical instruments.

Hands-on:
MAKE A PAROL

People in the Philippines decorate their homes with brightly coloured stars called *parols*. Make your own *parol* to add some more colour to your home this Christmas.

What you need

- scissors
- empty cereal box
- glue
- tissue paper
- strips of ribbon
- paper plate (optional)

What to do

1. With an adult's help, cut the cereal box into five strips. Each strip should be 2.5 centimetres (1 inch) wide and 38 cm (15 inches) long.
2. Glue two strips together at one end to form a flat V shape. Repeat with two other strips.
3. Place one V so that its open end faces to the right. Overlap the first V with the second V, so that the bottom ends connect. The point of the second V will form the top of your star. Use the last strip to connect the open ends. Glue all ends together.
4. Spread a thin layer of glue around your star's frame. Place a piece of tissue paper over the star. Allow this to dry and repeat on the other side. When dry, trim off extra paper.
5. Glue ribbon strips to the points of the star. You can also glue your *parol* to a paper plate before hanging it.

GLOSSARY

bamboo tropical grass with a hard, hollow stem

Christian person who follows a religion based on the teachings of Jesus. Christians believe that Jesus is the son of God.

evergreen tree or bush that has green leaves all year round

fiesta holiday or religious festival, especially in Spanish-speaking countries

ornament decoration hung on a Christmas tree

Three Kings three kings who are said to have followed a star to find Jesus in Bethlehem

READ MORE

Big Book of Christmas Decorations to Cut, Fold and & Stick, Fiona Watt (Usborne Publishing Ltd, 2013)

Christmas (Holidays and Festivals), Nancy Dickmann (Raintee, 2011)

Room for a Little One: The Story of Christmas, Martin Waddell (Orchard Books, 2015)

WEBSITE

www.bbc.co.uk/newsround/15790210

Learn about some more Christmas traditions from around the world.

INDEX